D1594720

EFFACEMENT

ELIZABETH

ARNOLD

EFFACEMENT

FLOOD EDITIONS 2010

Published by Flood Editions

floodeditions.com

ISBN 978-0-9819520-2-4

Design and composition by Quemadura
Cover photograph: Emmet Gowin,
Off-Road Traffic Pattern, Along the Northwest
Shore of the Great Salt Lake, Utah, 1988
Copyright Emmet and Edith Gowin
Courtesy Pace/MacGill Gallery, New York
Printed on acid-free, recycled paper
in the United States of America

This book was made possible in part
through a grant from the Illinois Arts Council

FIRST EDITION

Erthë tok of erthe erthë wyth wogh,
Erthe other erthë to the erthë drogh,
Erthë leyde erthe in erthënë throgh,
Tho hevëde erthe of erthe erthe ynogh.

ANONYMOUS

To a body anything can happen,
Like a brick.

GEORGE OPPEN

EFFACEMENT

I. AFTER PHILIP JOHNSON'S GLASS HOUSE

It could be air, a seemingly postless porch on a ridge edge in Connecticut.
Grounded by the too-wide dark brick cylinder within it?

Low clump of cabinets to the left
standing alone, no walls to be attached to. So

freestanding but not free.
Huddled.

As if round-backed, they're bent against the sky.
With everything exposed, they might find safety only

in that, and in their reddish, homey-colored wood.
But the corners are sharp, right-angled.

There's no hammer beam or sally in the house.
No gusset needed, balk. If there are sleepers, they're sunk.

Only the cylinder is curved, only that
having anything to do with what might bend toward imperfection.

Anatolian cuneiforms etched into it? —a cylinder seal to be rolled onto
lake-sized sheets of wax intaglio, a communication thus

entering the mind? But the ancient seals are a little bit
bowed, this isn't, smokestack shadow cast across the scene—

to scare off anyone who might approach
(as if they'd see it!) a room-sized house hanging in thin air,

banks of lush or leafless wild shrubs all around and down
the great ridge (for Connecticut)

may as well be in it. Trees erase it.

II.

You step down between
inward-inclining, heavily bulged

walls of earth.

J. Bell cries out to nothing
but unresponsive, narrowing earth,

no one before him

where the way loses its identity
in a network of watery ditches.

The prison of earth.

III.

Trenches across the face of France
filled in now, the surface sewn

—crenellated, to stop shots going
straight down the line.

Coronal suture arcing across the skull's hood with its
tongue-and-groove-edged bone plates joined,

frontal to parietal, parietal to occipital,
to shield the mysterious weave

of dendrites and their endless-seeming axons
lining the live bone underneath.

IV.

"Who openeth the dore of the face?"
"The effacing fingers of death."

V. AUTOBIOGRAPHY OF THE BODY

I wanted out, believed I had the right!

Back to the body thrust.
Like the people in New Orleans in their attics

flooded almost to the top,

no tool to break through
to the open night, not enough strength to swim

down through the house.

The aortic valve shot, surgery impossible,
scar-thickened heart rim's barrier (from the radiation)

better than the ribs to keep them out.

Inside, the heart beating too fast,
trying to get the blood flow up, my heart!

But one beat's labored, the other slurred,

everything sliding
even as it's scrambling

up the wet clay bank.

VI.

Imprisonment.
And inside that,

solitary.

For eleven years.
One can adjust to this, they say, but not

from it.

VII.

Entering earth, the soldiers do not hesitate
and, as if fearing punishment,

move forward in a line into position

quickly, glancing up like birds, down at their
buttons, boots—as much as they can see of them

in the mud—then back up fitfully in the film clip

cycling its short loop on the screen
embedded in an upper wall of the Tate,

the old technology hurrying them further.

They seem excited, like death-camp prisoners
filmed thirty years later, clothed or unclothed

as exposed.

VIII.

Inside a round-topped doorless doorway off loud Fleet Street,
on the broad floor of the circular twelfth-century nave of the Templars'
    church,

lie eight bodies. The deep-toned minute-paned stained glass
jewels the uneven pavement. Carved to last, unlike most bodies,

there's no pomp, no pedestal, inscription,
just effigies of earls and knights littered on the ground like us.

Eroded by time, the Blitz, one face looks scraped—it could hold
    rainwater like a bowl!
The one next door, meaty by comparison, rests its huge head on a
    plumped stone pillow.

Some don't have feet, one's leg's gone to the knee, more noses gone,
    a cheek.
Shields held at each left side—sharp!—don't help.

Stone dogs snuggle under their Achilles' heels.

IX.

With mountaintop-removal, valley-fill mining
they clear the trees first

then proceed to surgery.
The rubble from it chokes the streams.

X. CASE 76

Gunman W——, wounded in France 16.9.16, admitted
30.9.16, whole of intervening jaw missing. On the right side

stumps remaining, the whole of the upper lip and the whole
chin swept away, the tongue adherent to the margin

of the wound, three months later the first plastic done, a
large volcanic artificial chin attached by a splint to the upper

teeth, attempt to make a new mouth over this, the result
indifferent, no attempt to remake the chin carried out. Had it

been possible to retain the appliance, a satisfactory mouth
might have eventually been obtained, but the swinging in

of the flap on the left side caused considerable tension of the
new lip, and it was decided to remove the prosthesis, close

the lower opening to prevent dribbling. The intermediate-
stage photographic records (now missing) showed widening

of the mouth to the left so that access to the buccal cavity
could be obtained by the dental surgeon, Captain Fry,

working in conjunction with Sir Francis Farmer, who designed
an appliance to next stretch forward the tissues of the chin,

which had become more amenable to traction. The patient,
however, was not particularly tolerant to this procedure, and

I felt that perhaps one was wasting time, and, after consul-
tation with Sir Francis Farmer and Captain Fry, who advised

one to carry out a more radical procedure for the building up
of a new chin, the author obtained from Lieutenant W. W.

Edwards, the sculptor, a kind of chin in plaster the size of
a prosthesis necessary to make a chin over it. Around this

artificial apparatus was built an epithelial pouch: three
skin flaps reflected and sutured over the middle raw surface

outwards, flaps accurately designed beforehand in tinfoil.
The raw area thus created by the turning in of these skin flaps,

including the prominence of the new chin, accurately gauged
beforehand, a model cut in rolled-out lead plate, to which

were added the necessary pedicles, a large double-pedicle
scalp flap down to the chin. It all healed by first intention,

the pedicles being carefully attached—sewn skin edge to
skin edge, the central portion of the scalp skin-grafted, the

Thiersch grafts being taken from a tattoo mark in his right
forearm, the idea being that the blue mark would show

less conspicuously than white skin. It is interesting to note
that this mark contained the letters b-e-r-t and up to the

time of writing, six months after the operation, the letters
are still quite clearly legible on the top of this patient's scalp,

the original scalp skin swung via pedicle graft along and below
the chin and lower denture to the remains of the mandible,

no crinkling or retraction of the grafted scalp flap occurring now
—three months after the operation—and a satisfactory beard

could be easily grown. The patient, however, prefers to shave.

XI.

The radiation machine
didn't hum. The lights in the room dimmed.

Rads went through my chest
without a word.

         It took about a

half-hour
every day all summer.

XII.

What pokes out gets hit.
Statues tossed

by the hordes, by

anyone angry in an empty city,
knocked from

pedestals, high gables,

and a nose falls and
what's draped.

Everything—the bulging leaf,
rivery stone cloth

—off.

A young one lost his,
hole with a tube's all.

The nurse

cried. He
recovered.

XIII. CASE 151

Before reconstructive surgery
the soldiers' eyes

look like theirs.

Even in distress it's their distress.
One man: beautiful,

though everything below the nose on one side's gone

and the nose itself
wounded,

as was determined later,

beyond repair.
When it was reinvented with the jaw,

the man's eyes

(though untouched)
hardened.

Everything he was went with the surgeries.

The result:
satisfactory.

XIV.

The skin grafts looked like ridges, one like a bluff.

XV.

A man Henry Tonks drew
medical illustrations of

can't close his mouth

because he doesn't have a mouth,
the right jaw gone, the chin.

In the eyes, there is a face.

I put my hand over the wound to see
less of the trying to be good,

more resignation.

The eyes alive in a dead face
soon will join it

as the surgeons fail,

mouth after mouth a mess,
the slightest slant

throwing everything off,

a pleading look
stamped, permanently wincing

while the eyes say something else—

XVI.

What subtle brain's meanderings are
cut, crimped

—death of a thought, a
way of thinking

definite in its pattern as a profile.

XVII. PICTURES

Hot, late June in London, sunny for a change, and the air
missing some of its oxygen apparently.

I breathed it, got lost walking
past Westminster Abbey in a no man's land of

houses mixed with office buildings, squares with grocers, kids, then
nothing but unpopulated dirt-encrusted tomb-like dead ends.

"Go," she said. "If you like Bacon you'll love Freud."

But the paintings broke their banks—bodies
mottled, obese, seemed to be swimming

through some kind of slop across three yards of canvas,
faces and torsos, vulvas, cocks,

no cube or disc chalked over them, as in Bacon's best,
nothing to counter flesh.

Then Tonks' delicately drawn cracked soldiers' faces
in another, smaller room—

as he depicted them.

The way a genius mind turns into something
other than a self, Tonks turned

to the that-which-can't-be-fooled
as he stroked the paper, looked up, saw

shapes instead of faces

                           —and the eyes,

eyes of gurus-in-the-making pleading.

It took a self like that, a non- or second self
—already dead! said Marcus Aurelius.

As he depicted them:

beings caught out of ordinary living.
Offerings themselves though left alive,

what could they do but, face after face, look

at us
as they did at Tonks.

At us now *via* Tonks
longingly.

        For understanding
(with little expectation of it)

of what they had become past what they looked like

                                          —that was the door!

Those who survived, that is, who
didn't lose their minds, the ones who could still

follow orders, sit.
A camera would have missed it.

XVIII.

In the early universe, it was light that formed
the dominant constituent, and ordinary matter played

only the role of a negligible contamination.

XIX. PICTURES (II)

They sat me up in the bed—no, had me stand
on the cold tile floor while the plastic surgeon drew

black magic-marker hash marks on my chest

—as sixteen years before the radiologists did
in burnt-orange

before the bluish pinprick tattoos (still there)

were applied, marking the radiation field
twenty-two years before the second plastic surgeon

and his aid laughed mixing colors for the nipple patch

which, nine years after that, has faded
almost completely.

They wanted me to have a life, and the ones before them

life
    —why can't I concentrate on that

stirring fact?

Instead of the all that plagues me daily

                                       —that

    enormity.

XX.

I couldn't hear them
because I couldn't see

their faces at the table
the morning I lost my glasses.

I couldn't
see, I

couldn't understand
what they were saying.

At parties, Joyce took off his glasses,
chose it, not to see.

As if he could then not be seen.
He let himself believe it.

XXI. HANGING FIRE (SUSPECTED ARSON)

The fire over except its end, except how

anything physical keeps ending
forwards or backwards

—here
both:

the charred pieces of wood from a burnt-down woodshed
hang on strings

invisible enough for a story,

story of a loss, the beauty of suspension that includes the loss,
while the bigger flame-shaped pieces,

darker seeming for their greater mass,
are near the bottom of the

cubed rectangle of wood and air

not a foot above the ground and at the top,
about a foot below the ceiling that's suffused with light,

black-black against that
the smaller, higher-up chips of the top two-thirds float

asteroid-belt distanced, weightless.

While reassembling the sculpture at the ICA in Boston,
something she had done before

and with other, similar works,
Cornelia Parker said:

"They look like corpses when they're on the ground."

XXII.

There were too many idle days at Aldershot.
Tonks grew tired, went off with delight

to Hill Hall at Christmas,
did drawings of Mrs. Hunter and her grandchildren.

"A very agreeable change from jaws."

XXIII. CASE 517

5.3.18. *Operation.*—Rhinoplasty, subtotal Indian method.

16.4.18. *Operation.*—Right costal cartilage implantation. Two large pieces put in for nose and eye. Skin grafts over the undisturbed granulations. A piece of whole-thickness skin the size of a florin put in.

Result.—Satisfactory.

8.6.18. *Operation.*—A piece of cartilage taken from subcutaneous store, shaped in form of rod and inserted from the root of the nose.

Result.—Satisfactory.

27.6.18. *Operation.*—Further implantation to give form to the tip. A third main piece inserted between the skin and the previous cartilage rod, which gave a very fine-edged bridge effect. An eyelid plastic performed at the same sitting.

Result.—No trouble occurred.

But on the eighth day an abscess formed, the last bridge cartilage evacuated. On the eighth day the nose suppurated and had to be re-opened. Pus and the last bridge cartilage were evacuated. On the eighth day, the nose was obliterated from within.

18.10.18. *Operation.*—Transfer of piece of cartilage from No. 681 for future use.

18.12.18. *Operation.*—The above piece of cartilage inserted in tip and bridge.

Result.—Healed.

XXIV.

As recorded in the ancient *Sushruta Samhita,* the sacred medical record
(in three volumes) of the Hindoos

focusing on surgical procedures (mostly inspired by war), full-thickness
free
skin grafts were used along with

pedicle flaps for nasal reconstruction by the Kooman caste of tile and
brick makers,
free full-thickness skin grafts

being harvested from the gluteal region and applied to the nasal defect.
Oribasius later recommended

flap surgery in his seventy-volume *Synagogue Medicae* (over half of
which is lost)
to keep up the blood supply.

Justinian II had a forehead-flap procedure to repair his nose, mutilated
to prevent
reascension to the throne. It

helped that Galen was monotheistic, but surgery was considered manual
    labor

and thus dropped once Christianity

gave way to the mysticism of the Middle Ages.

XXV. IRAQI BOY

What appear to be
peach-white, overwashed pajamas

in the washed-out newspaper photo

on one side droop
like a monk's hood,

the upper half of that leg

raised with the other whole one
and the hands

they're there!

and the less washed-out
pink balloon above them that they reach for or have

just let go

—the latter probably as one hand, palm up,
is wide of it,

two-thirds of a laughing mouth

visible, the wheelchair in this case,
its sparkle stark against

the flannel and plied living limbs within it,

a tool of fun. Such wisdom's possible here only,
the ability to feel

glad to be alive

gone on the outside,
the "cloistered incarceration" of the ward

holding the boys

as if they were a group of monks.
Asked by a visitor

what it's like to live secluded

most of the time,
mute and with forced labor,

a chronic lack of sleep for all the praying,

the Benedictine monk
asked back:

"Have you ever been in love?"

XXVI. AFTER GEORG BASELITZ

A woman's body aped in putty,
gray and black, some yellow

—*Bildachtundzwanzig (No Birds).*

It's tilting down or
over to the left, gravity-pulled

and starting to tip, to fall

her full weight down, down
or over. She's a heavy body only,

her hair not long enough to strum.

XXVII.

When Virgil saw me stand there
unmoved and stubborn before the Purgatorial flame,

he said, a little vexed,
"Now see, between Beatrice and you is this wall."

XXVIII.

A friend or lover,
friend with the spark that could send things further,

seeming to be made of rubber when the wall goes up
between us at the table.

The mind protects the mind.

Wall of plexiglass (can he see it?) or of
flesh displaced—the

that which blinds perceivers

to whatever it is that can't help wanting
to get through. I

want to, to move

drowningly toward the other
for the time it takes to see he isn't seeing what a body needs to

to desire. It's just

bodies

that will always block that,

the visibly significantly marred ones

more. Mine,

not me

      —right?

How much of a self is skin?

XXIX.

.

Below the boundaryless mid-ocean
where the lit part blurs into the hadal depths,

thin-skinned fish float
as in a scientist's suspension in a lab,

various tints of bioluminescence lighting them
to various degrees of brightness

in the dark, clear water—clear as air!—
but dark, dark as a night you'd stumble through,

the clarity apparent
only from the colors of the

mostly exposed, seemingly weightless bodies
pushing hard from the inside

to hold their shapes against
the volumes of water (a ton for every centimeter)

pushing in.
       That they can take that—

pressure's the air they breathe!
—while busy doing everything possible to trick outsiders:

the googly-eyed glass squid
going from long-thin to spherical,

and if that doesn't work
it draws its head in, bleeds black ink into its body,

including the fibrous densities of the bright white eyestalks,
disappears.

XXX.

At Aldershot, the nurses took the mirrors
off the ward walls

before they came, before they woke up.

XXXI.

Delusions, stories
heal, Freud said.

Believe, believe.

I dreamed
I had another's body

trying on a nylon dress at the mall,

the pounding heat outside
over as the cool cloth

slipped down

the narrow column of me
in the air conditioning.

XXXII.

There is no doubt the gunners have a
much better time of it than the infantry. They

certainly live in greater peace and comfort,
and their particular method of killing

men is full of scientific interest. As we passed
one of the batteries we found them engaged

in a game of football. Suddenly the
sharp sound of a whistle was heard

and in a moment every man was a motionless
statue. A hostile aeroplane overhead would

at once have detected the gun position if the
men had been moving, whereas motionless

they are invisible. We stood thus for a couple of
minutes, and then two blasts were sounded

on the whistle, and we were free to move again.

XXXIII.

Mask on, and a shirt, I move among those
who require them.

As a mirror does,
mirror I once sought all candor from

—not about my body only,
but as when something

inner joins the surface, sings, speaks.

XXXIV.

In the whistlers' room, no words go
from face to face.

The mouths look good
but every throat is bandaged.

They manage,
whistling through their neck straws, happy

the way child-twins who speak invented words are
until every communicative sound shrivels

in the superheated air outside their circle.

XXXV.

After twenty surgeries, the boy died. They'd
rushed things; he couldn't wait

to see in the mirror someone's face.

XXXVI.

I'd sit by the aquarium awhile, a girl enthralled, waiting for the fish
to lose their fear, regain their colors, swim

freely, pleasing me. I was happy to be gone.

XXXVII. MONSTER

An eye-shaped patch from my upper back

—something like Picasso's
in *Les Demoiselles d'Avignon* or *Woman in a Hairnet,*

kid-crayon boat, my skin still tanned
from growing up on the water in north Florida—

transferred to the front, sewn onto skin that's whiter.

Poor monster. He had skin from *others*—corpses!—
right from the start.

Everybody ran or, if cornered,
hit him. He was a

man, a person,

full-grown, infant-minded,
lying in the lean-to with the

hole in the wall that joined it to the house,

invisible membrane
—like an eye's!—

all that divided him from a life,
world of the close-knit family he took as his own

until they saw him.

He'd been free
to learn how to live by watching.

As in the woods below the moon he'd learned—
open, animal

—until he saw himself.

Frankenstein saw the eyes
open—

It was too much to imagine
a soul in that

and he couldn't name him.

Without a name there's no
entity

to hold against its own cells'
multiple dividings past itself,

nothing of what we started as
materially.

●

What if everyone were eyeless
and we could only

hear, feel space,

so that that feeling eclipsed seeing,
roared it to the side?

Old men's voices, chanting, channeling,
choruses in cathedrals

—you have to close your eyes to see it.

●

The sound of the *gueule cassée*'s voice
only made things harder

for the boy, who hadn't seen his father since he'd
been struck by artillery.

He knew the voice, the walk and other subtle gestures,
hints caught every instant in the

incremental process of perception.
Knowing him made the marred face even worse

just as the monster's human traits had made him
more of a monster to his maker

or anyone who saw him.

●

The soldier dreamed he was a clay jar,
the kind shaped like a female body.

Had he been hit? He didn't know.
He stood in clay.

Spring came, but with the trees eviscerated,
you could tell the Earth moved forward

only by the birds, the cold's
momentary incinerations.

                           ●

". . . space as medium rather than
container."

The body as that?

That through which we are
no matter what the shape, the scars.

                           ●

To appear, to shine
is to be a face.

Effacement's closer to death, the face
wingless,

nothing but a wing.

                           ●

Prodigy, divine

omen

—*monstri*

see more, warn us.

XXXVIII.

Questo muro. Wall of light, of fire.
To believe it won't hurt walking a heavy body

through that out of Purgatory!

XXXIX.

In the mornings I woke up to light
shimmering off the river on my bedroom wall.

It digitally jerked sometimes so fast it flowed,

then scattered for an instant,
then resumed.

I *was* that light, my cells dividing
into my becoming,

cells of light!

—and the wall
loosening, dissolving . . .

Then someone walked in without knocking, talking.

XL.

I reached a point, a pivot,
thinking I'd turned

outward
once and for all, away

—it's looking out that's living—
then saw Muir's report:

"There is one perturbing
experience that's inevitable. It's

this. He (the nurse) finds he must
fraternize with his fellow men

at whom he cannot look
without the grievous task

of betraying by his expression
how awful is their appearance.

I confess that this discovery

came as a surprise.

I had not known before

how usual and necessary

a thing it is to gaze

straight at anybody

to whom one is speaking,

and to gaze with

no embarrassment

when some unguarded glance of yours

may cause him hurt."

XLI.

You can see more as a soul,
darkness speeding into darkness.

Earth's harder.

Like a spacecraft on reentry,
the body has to

burn its way through the sky's lens.

XLII. PHENOMENOLOGY
OF PERCEPTION

Merleau-Ponty says the body is
"the manner in which an I

comes to know and express itself.

My experience breaks forth into things,
things that are not my things.

World, world, definition of my body
—how I come to know and express myself."

◉

"The soule is delighted with variety.
It is dulled with identity."

◉

Which to trust,
a categorizing, disbelieving spirit

such as Aristotle's,

or that which
purposing or not

glows
into what's before it,

goes

spreading

flows?

XLIII.

Four in the morning, working to stop
the voices talking

in my head, with the marred heart
racing, skipping beats,

I take deep breaths and
suddenly

I'm in the ophthalmologist's darkened exam room
forty years back

and the phoroptor lens drops,
clicks inside its casing,

and the whole world shifts,
then another, thicker lens, then

                                        nothing

—heart of the mind, heart in a body,
body in a house in the troposphere

where all our weather is,

three men—alive!—in the half-shattered *Odyssey*,

Apollo 13, third mission to the moon they had to
sling their ship around instead of landing.

Huddling in the too-small, frayed tinfoil hull
of the LEM they'd moved to,

they forced the roughshod manual burns
to steer

computerless at apogee

aiming themselves themselves
at the bowling-ball-hard black-blue planet

and the sea Odysseus was whirled around in
by the gods.
            My father stood

on the heaving deck of the submarine chaser,
a Coast Guard cutter

but not full length, scant ordnance,
and the other larger ship they'd tried to guard

hit, sunk
before the destroyer radioed

made it to the scene,
the depth charges having

fallen onto nothing.

Helpless as Odysseus minus the gods,
my father and the others watched

the sea fill up with men,
room only for a few in their boat.

Helpless as Odysseus *with* the gods,
Tiresias lapping up the blood.

The destroyer came in time to save my father,
or maybe the U-boat just

swam away in the murk . . .

And a year before he died in the loony bin,
the woman sitting across the room screamed

"Help!"

for the hundred and twenty-seventh time that morning.

XLIV.

In a freezer when I read it he was
probably gray.

My sister saw his body turn gray
as he died, then suddenly

grayer.
          Now what color is it?

Not so deep in the ground as I'd thought,
the concrete, swimming-pool-like vault

halting for a little while the give of earth.
I want to be against earth

bodily, I said.
As against you in our bed, Jack.

XLV.

A wisp of thought being all we've got.

White-throated sparrow's single flute-note
at the start, the hermit thrush's . . .

Those rare occasions we link.

You there with your hand out,
your fingers fiddling

like a barnacle's feathery body reaching
from its shell

into the river water.

A face brightening, being transformed.
Your face being.

What's left of what I love.

XLVI. AFTER THE STORM

By the path to the salmon run,
the stream out of hearing up the trail in a park outside Olympia,

a flock of winter wrens
hopped and fluttered in the undergrowth.

It was as if they'd just arrived
out of the nest together,

a couple of dozen emerging
as if cellularly

—more like cubs than birds,
liquid clumps.

But the salmon held firm in their bodies,
black and white like cows

but missile-shaped, a little bit of silver.
Some swam in groups, others alone.

They struggled in loud water just to keep from going backwards
after the storm. Worn out, solitary

whether alone or not, they inched upstream,
fell back, wavered forward, nosed

at the big dark underwater parts of rocks, cozying up to them
their only friends.

XLVII.

Heyerdahl's men saw they were
of it, of the

sky, sea,

the balsa logs their raft was made of
growing seaweed as it floated

quietly over the Pacific,

a reef of fish in the shaded world
under it, the guitar above, books, art.

"Bonitos swam onboard with the waves."

NOTES AND ACKNOWLEDGMENTS

Poem II uses sentences from David Jones' *In Parenthesis*. Poem IV uses quotations found in the *OED*. Poems X and XXIII use words and sentences from Harold Gillies' 1920 study, *Plastic Surgery of the Face*. Poem XIII is a response to photographs from that book. Aldershot, England preceded Sidcup as the center for plastic reconstructive surgery on British WWI soldiers with facial wounds. Gillies ran both centers. Poem XVIII is out of Steven Weinberg's *The First Three Minutes: A Modern View of the Origin of the Universe*. Poem XXII quotes from a letter by Henry Tonks. Poem XXIV draws on various histories of surgical practices of ancient India. I quote from Patrick Leigh Fermor's *A Time to Keep Silence* at the end of poem XXV. In poems XXVII and XXXVIII, I quote from Charles Singleton's translation of Dante's *Purgatorio*. Poem XXIX borrows words and phrases from Claire Nouvian's *The Deep*. Poem XXXII is drawn from William Boyd's *With a Field Ambulance at Ypres: Being Letters Written March 7–August 15, 1915*. Poem XXXIV refers to a German hospital ward of WWI soldiers with throat wounds who communicated by whistling through their tracheotomy tubes, as described by Paul Alverdes in *Die Pfeiferstube*. The fifth section of poem XXXVII draws on a story told in Henriette Remi's *Hommes sans visage*. The French phrase "gueule cassée" means "cracked face." French soldiers with facial wounds were called this. The seventh section of XXXVII quotes the archaeologist Christopher Tilley. In poem XL, I quote Ward Muir, a journalist who wrote about Sidcup during the war. In the second section of poem XLII, I use quotations from the *OED*. Poem XLVII refers to *Kon-Tiki*, in which Thor Heyerdahl chronicles his 1947 journey in a large, unmotorized raft of pre-Columbian design 3,770 nautical miles across the Pacific from Peru to Raroia, a Polynesian island. Heyerdahl made the trip to prove a theory about prehistoric emigration patterns in that part of the world.

Versions of poems in this book first appeared in *At Length*, *Berkeley Review*, *Chicago Review*, *Gulf Coast*, *Literary Imagination*, *Paris Review*, *Poetry*, and *Smartish Pace*. Poem I appeared in the 2010 *Alhambra Poetry Calendar* and was included in Baltimore's CityLit Project. Woodland Pattern Bookstore made a broadside out of poem XLVII.

Thanks to colleagues and friends, especially Lindsay Bernal, Michael Collier, Liz Countryman, Lisa McCullough, Stan Plumly, Tom Sleigh, and Josh Weiner, for their help with many of the poems and, in some cases, the book as a whole. Thanks also to the editors of Flood, Devin Johnston and Michael O'Leary, whose well of patience, intelligence, and stamina is apparently bottomless. Stella Mason, former Keeper of the College Collections at the Royal College of Surgeons of England, granted me access to Henry Tonks' drawings and provided background information on Tonks' life. Andrew Bamji, who oversees the Gillies Archive at Sidcup Hospital outside London, provided a crucial bibliography of books and articles on this subject, as well as his own unpublished translation of a chapter of Henriette Remi's *Hommes sans visage*. Many thanks also to the Rockefeller Foundation, the Ucross Foundation, and the University of Maryland's College of Arts and Humanities for their generous support. Special thanks go to Jack, and for the world we've made.

INDEX OF TITLES AND FIRST LINES

Elizabeth Arnold's other books are *The Reef* (University of Chicago Press, 1999) and *Civilization* (Flood Editions, 2006). Her poems have appeared in *Conjunctions*, *Paris Review*, *Poetry*, and *Slate*. She is on the MFA faculty at the University of Maryland and lives in Hyattsville, Maryland.